SCOTTISH POETRY 8

A

SCOTTISH POETRY 8
an anthology

edited by
MAURICE LINDSAY
ALEXANDER SCOTT
RODERICK WATSON

A Carcanet Press publication
with the support of the Scottish Arts Council

First published 1975 by
Carcanet Press Limited
266 Councillor Lane
Cheadle Hulme, Cheadle
Cheshire SK8 5PN

Printed in Great Britain
by Eyre & Spottiswoode Limited at Grosvenor Press,
Portsmouth

Preface

While we are appearing under a new imprint, our editorial policy remains as in the previous volume, and this anthology represents a selection of work submitted and poems published in periodicals during the last year.

It is sad that in the last twelve months three poets have died, Helen B. Cruickshank at the age of 89, Sydney Goodsir Smith at 59, and Charles Senior at 56. They will be greatly missed.

Once again we acknowledge our indebtedness to the Scottish Arts Council, and to the following publications from which we have chosen poems:

Akros, Blackwood's Magazine, Encounter, Lines, The New Review, New Statesman, The Observer, The Scotsman, Scottish Literary Journal, Scotia Review, and *The Times Literary Supplement.*

Our thanks are due to Miss Lindsey MacLeod for the sub-editorial work on this volume.

Submissions for *Scottish Poetry 9* should be sent to The Scottish Civic Trust, 24 George Square, Glasgow, to whom we are indebted for this facility.

Contents

David Angus
CALVIN ON WARK

It disna hae tae profit ye
Or ony-yin,
Or dae ony guid that
Ony-yin kin see.
It maunna gie ye pleesure —
That smacks (ye ken) o leesure.
It's best wioot aa thae things, ye'd agree.

The main thing is — ye *thole* it
As ye dae it,
An wioot thae things ye thole it
Mair an mair.
Ye plodder an ye ploiter,
Ye swat an strain an stoiter,
An whit it's aa about ye binna shair.

But the main thing is — ye *thole* it;
Yon's a guid thing.
The sinfu flesh is punishin
Itsel.
The waur it feels, the better.
Ye're het? Ye culd be hetter.
It's hellish — but it keeps ye out o Hell!

David Black
POEM TO PROPOSE THE CANONISING OF DAVID HUME
(Whose name has been given to one of the main towers of the
new Edinburgh University buildings in George Square.)

Neither Christ on the road to Calvary nor the
Buddha under his bodhidendron could have
quite approved of you, David Hume, the titular
deity now of my recent educators:
yet indeed for myself I come increasingly
to esteem that controlled mind, cool head but by
no means fusionless energy, both met in a
body like a construction of stiff cushions
and a manner composed to keep what might be di-
sturbing minimal: no one takes such pains for

11

nothing, nor with so good a brain and in an
age of conscious Enlightenment claims repeatedly,
'Reason is and should only be the slave of
Passion'! — startling opinion, that we owe not to the
paunchy epicure who on introspecting to
find his faults could discover only a certain
weakness for the society of (wasn't it?)
'modest women', but to a voider vision
seen, I choose to believe, and not rejected
out of cowardice but for love of living —
call it vanity, gourmandise, or trivial
irresponse to the call to be authentic
if you prefer. Of course in here proposing
we enrol you among the beatified I
am embarked on an odder enterprise than
often, yet one would hardly question that the
two chief qualifications you surprisingly
adequately fulfil: firstly the Vision,
for the universe rendered One if only
in a homogeneity of evanishing
particles has of itself the verve and majesty
I would seek in a God (and in dissolving the
Self I need not point out you even gain the
peak of Union!); and, in addition (the
fact of my writing this poem proves it fairly), you
let it seem life is worth the comic baffling
exploration the likes of us are fated
not to emerge from but (Heaven defending) maybe to
learn in the end some love for. And what are Saints? a
                                          question
the wise man would have got to sooner) — I think
they must do the above; and then become en-
grossing subjects of speculation, and (I su-
spect supremely) they must be made an ikon.
— Our role, David! ignoring your confusion.

Alan Bold
AMONG THE RAINDROPS

A spider's web sprayed with raindrops
Stretches over deep black crumbling soil
And sparkles like a field of polished diamonds

And glistens like a spun prism of dropped colour;
Tottering on the water-laden fine wire blanket
The acrobatic tightrope-walking spider
Stops and shakes itself, shakes itself and stops
Until a way is cleared among the labyrinthine traps
Each tightrope section represents.
                              A fly descends
Almost to be drowned by the overwhelming blur
Of coloured undulating water. Drenched wings knit
And panic-stricken life-deserting puny legs of wire
Interweave reluctantly with life-exhausting lengths of wire.

FENCES

Even in nature man makes divisions,
Mapping out territorial acquisitions
With stones that fence out fields and grass
As solid warnings against trespass.
Yet sheep in winter wear frozen cones of wool
That tinkle like pieces of steel.
And the animals refuse to be fenced in.
These stupid sheep blunder, baa out their din
And stupidly stray from their territory.
   This, of course, is allegory
In reverse. The sheep are sick
Of imitating man who likes to stick
To the bit he was born to,
Never wonderingly wandering into blue
Grass or green skies but instead
Fencing fields inside his head —
(Never seeing grass running like a green sea,
Rivers drifting into eternity,
Buttercups shaking their yellow heads,
Thistles bursting out of earthbound beds,
The erratic arrow of the swift
Winging its way through a wind drift)
— Fencing fields inside his head
And staying there.

The sheep flutter into the air.

Alex S. Borrowman
PENELOPE

Sae dowf for puir Penelope!
Her man, Odysseus gaed awa tae weir,
And focht ten year afore the waas o Troy,
Wi nine year mair stravaigin owre the sea.
Maist twenty year! the while she set at hame
And span her wab, like onie wife in Thrums!
Focht aff the wooers; mindit — whiles — her man,
Redd up the hoose, and dreed the nichts herlane.

Owre dowf for puir Penelope!
Stownlins her man, Odysseus cam hame
Frae anters vast in lands ayont the sea.
He spak o Circe, and o douce Nausicaa
And o yon nymph Calypso, fidgin fain
For him tae bide wi her upon Ogygia.
He spak! Sae dowf for puir Penelope
Wha hadna lain aspar for nineteen year!

Derek Bowman
DURHAM MARKET

First entering a market housed
In far too small
A building the whole
City seemed eagerly to flow

Down into. The constantly being
Pulled hither
And thither
By mercenary daughters towards

Guinea-pigs, mice, birds — such creatures
As cower
Under straw
Or flutter about in cages.

Jostled all the time by shoppers.
The sevenpenny
Trumpery
Rings we found we had to buy the girls

14

From some magpie of a woman
(One glass stone
Dropped out even
As they passed the counter).

The corner graveyard of mouldering
Books, a hiss
And flare of gas-
Light rembrandting the yawning

Sacristan. — Glancings, impulse buys,
Market touches
That caress
The memory. But still seeping

Deep into my mind those bilberries
An outside stall-
Keeper shovelled
Businesslike, poundwise into bags

From boxes of blue globes pressed so tight
Their juice came slipping
Through slats, dripping
Richness onto cobble-stones.

George Mackay Brown
SEA VILLAGE
(Stations of The Cross)

There he rides now. Look. The laird.
A brace of grouse to the Manse.
One hand on the rein long and white and scented.

Every boat in the voe is his, and the gear.
He fixes the price of the catch.
But a certain fisherman has laid his own keel.

The store? That's his too. After dark
It's a shebeen, with a crock
Of peatsmoke whisky. A man can drink till he falls.

The fisherman's mother bides here, a good woman.
No tramp takes a bitter mouth from her door.
It's her boy, Ollie Manson, that's building the boat.

The whole parish forbidden to help him.
But Simon left his threshing
And brought hammer and rivets down to the rock.

And Vera, whom he humped over the tarpot
Came with a jar from the burn.
His face flashed once in the gray water.

A black lamp in a window there. Look.
But after nightfall
Moths and men flutter her flame. The slut.

The five widows of the *Hopeful*
In this one threshold,
Rock-gathered, like stormbirds, head into wind.

Socialist books, that was the start of it.
I blame the dominie.
Paine and Blatchford, they'll bring him down.

It'll end with lawmen and prison.
They'll strip his eaves.
His mother will sit under a bare rooftree.

No need to tell you, with the clang and reek,
Who's shuttered here.
The blacksmith hammering nails for the Hall.

That's it now, on the noust, the *Equality*.
'The yawl is finished!'
The yawl is finished. More than a yawl is finished.

L. Smith, Joiner. Always a coffin on hand.
Never a smile on Lowrie
But when a window goes blind in some croft.

Up there, among the cornfields, the kirk
Cold as a sunk creel.
On a Sabbath, sea voices shake the stone.

George Bruce
UNDER THE MOON

The flowers that fringed the waves
waylaid, sucked his white body
in a wild wash, cut by sharp rocks.
This was the death of a swimmer,
a boy, in November, moonlit.
Lovers, walking on the sands, did not know
his time had run out, theirs being
fulfilled in hushing sound,
turning gently the shells on the beach.
She picked up a fan, a pink shell,
held it transparent before the moon.
'Love, put it in your pocket for me.'
He put her in his pocket. The waves
whisper in her shell ear, 'Love'.

CHOPIN AT 10 WARRISTON CRESCENT — 1848
(Alicia Danuta Fiderkiewicz — 1974)

It wis the cauld that got ye,
and yon twisty stairs; you sclimmin
them like yer hert tae burst,
Everest wi-oot oxygen tae you —
syne at the tap, the piano
an ootside leaves gan heilster-gowdie.
Ye were fair connach'd,
or sae we thocht, but some pooch
in yer hert had virr that ettled
tae win oot, an did, in your fingers
till thon hoose rocked in your thunner.
The siller leddies, hauns in their lap,
gied naething awa; the gents
lookt like stookies (and mebbe were)
but you soon't oot a' rooms an ha's
an ower a' watters tae Europe
an across the plains wi snaw
whaur merched the Poles, an
puir folk wi a' their wardly gear
upon the roads — thae refugees,
then an noo.

17

An so's your music
then an noo in a lassie's fingers,
makin sic steir, the air tremmlin,
speakin your leid, your folk's leid,
an oors, a' wha bide haudin
tae thenselves, that benmaist thing
that dwalls, waitin for the kinlin
till the spark loups at the hert.
Then a' the trash o' the warld's
forgot, a' the riff-raff wi naethin
i their heids but the neist kick
o' the ba that lang syne's burst.

'Tak hert' says your sang. The snaw
tummles on Scotland and you're awa.
'Maks nae odds. I'm in that sang
that soon't yestreen, the-day,
an will dae the-morn an a'.'

CHOPIN AT 10 WARRISTON CRESCENT — 1848
(For Alicja Danuta Fiderkiewicz — piantist — 1974)

Thunder and silver — the air trembling.

We came upstairs with the invalid Chopin
climbing the turning stairs, Everest without oxygen,
then taking all his heartache into his music,
blood on the stones of Wroclaw, memories
of his defiant country and its terrible history,
he put them down, inarticulate marks on a white sheet.

You, a girl, found his heart in your fingers.
The red deepens in the roses,
the dark rages outside the panes.
The refugees are taking to the roads, old guns fire;
despair rattled the bones of the frail man
at the piano, who was about you in that room.
'Remember,' he said, 'not a dying man — '
Dry leaves dance in the street,
in the salons mazurkas and polonaises,
the banners of liberty on the snow, scatter,
are taken into the future in a small room
in another country.

18

Tom Buchan
from ONWORDS

*

learn to fly
launch out on the unknown
every so often
take time out
spread your wings
and spread your wings
take a journey
launch out fearlessly
(or fearfully)
learn to fly
brandnew spaces
in your airyplane

*

you don't have to believe it but
out there in the unknown lately
give or take a few million years
a highly evolved species
so much more highly evolved than us it's hard if not
                                        impossible
to conceive
achieved enlightenment/breakthrough/rebirth
call it what you like
they don't have a word for it either
and the whole lot of them were about to evolve
beyond
beyond themselves
beyond the system
about to be altered and expanded/utterly changed
and instantaneously realised what some of them had
                                        always known
that proceeding for them would involve leaving us
behind
behind
unknowingly bereaved/even doomed to our status quo
extinction

so they collectively decided
(no long debates — millions of them perhaps)
stayed to live on meantime, believing
we and the others crucial

*

today I spent 2 hours
listening to raindrops on rowan leaves

then I walked up the hill in a mist
and was convinced that I was about to leave the planet

but came back in more than one piece

*

intuitions are not enough —
        sometimes I feel lonely that in my 70
        or whatever years
        I shall not comprehend everything
        experience *all* — could live to 1000
        and still not have enough time
        to understand the immediate neighbourhood

today
        now that the bracken has withered
        I discovered a new microcontinent
        a mysterious hollow 50 yards behind the house
        uprooted tree
        a strange assortment of stones
        yet every day for months I had passed within a
                               few feet of it

sat there for minutes
        in the warm November sun
        the sky a small circle above me
        populated by clouds crisscrossed by finches and
                             extending . . .
        and suddenly knew
        there is nothing 'behind' nature
        nothing concealed or encoded or secret

everything
        around and within us available to us
        waiting
        unconcernedly
        waiting for the skilled or naive intelligence, for the
                             dreamer
        for the clean awareness taken through puzzlement
        through and beyond itself

to the (how to express it?)
      diversity contained in the one many-dimensioned
      entity
      itself multipotential
      and only the beginning of the
      inexpressible
      beauty

*

strange house familiar house
houses we and I have lived in
impinged on by brickwork wallpapers and the dead
the roof for which all the owners
are collectively responsible
streets frantic with trauma traffic and parties

the comings and going of friends and tricky
visits of relatives the unrolling procession
of tenants marriages affairs murders separations
jobs ambitions madnesses the taut psychodramas all
                                      around
violent or quiet transience
and the kids' noisy politics

dead cul-de-sacs where you wake up under nitrozepam
to the far-off shudder of a latenight bus
$19 a week rooms with rotten Before Christ plumbing
where the light always fuses among dominant fridge smells
screams laughter shots in the night
and longdistance calls collect

priestly Mysors compound — goats munching neem leaves
crows gekkos and metallic
fluting of brilliantly plumaged birds
a stooping sudra sweeping the yellow grass
one hand behind his back and white brahmin cow
waiting patiently to be milked

the relaxing urban peace of council estates
o textures of pebbledash concrete and tufted carpet
where the gossip has almost died down for the day
and the hydrangea
perfects itself among gaudy pyjamas violet nylon sheets
and stimulating grafitti

and it's so heartwarming to contemplate the TV on its
                                                    castors
and know the sideboard's stuffed with lager and bitter
                                                    lemon
the mice coming out in daylight to eat the dog's food
— and what about the vast rolling claustrophobic pine-
                                        bordered lawns
of the very well-off
the long tastefully curving carefully stocked and weeded
                                                rockeries?

strange house familiar house our house my house
primitive house
though owned by someone else appropriate to me
which when we leave will be bereavement for me
bereavement for it
when all the cats we ever had are dead

what good thing happened here and when?
no evil comes
curative intriguing continuously satisfying
where the moss grows imperceptibly the wind's a comfort
and storms bring unfathomable reassurance —
house almost as exciting and calming as a new friend

snug boiled egg and toast which say
'this will go on for ever'
the unfolding process of lives change recurrence and rebirth
strange house familiar house
built not of stone but some kind of flesh
that lives

*   what a morning awakening!
and to think I might be dead by my own hand
or frenzied or jealous because my lover wanted to be free
or mouthing in front of cameras or students
or anxious about money
or hustling or politicking
or attempting to write literature
when here is the world superb
difficult work to be done
the first frost of the year
fox in the garden
frozen plums on the old tree
the children beginning to talk and move

my son is listening to sounds coming into his head
from space he says
I reassure him that he's right
and put my awareness out to him through the dawnlight

how precious the world is
I have fallen head over heels in love with life
links cohesions complexities puzzles elucidations
dramas explorations
walk out into the 50 mph sleet
and through a window of blue sky the regular plane
from Dusseldorf to Toronto contrails through cirrus
ruthless tender inevitable journey
surprises all the way

Donald Campbell
IN THE TENEMENT O MY MIND

Somewhaur
in the tenement o my mind
an immigrant Pole
is playin a piece bi Chopin
on the piano — only I'm no jist shair
o the exact composition. A woman
wi curlers in her hair
is hammerin hell out of her hall cairpet
in the back green.

Atween the lichtsome lilt o melody
and the reid-raw rhythm o necessity
there's anither sound;
a harmony I can haurdly hear
a kinna threnody
that thrums awa
in the darkness o the stair.

THE WINDS O JANUARY

Just as if they kent
Just as is they'd heard frae history
The winds o January
blaw boisterous and bauld
owre aa creation, owre aa our warld.

It's a time
for cleanin out and reddin up.
The winds come
to clear the debris and time awa
the aff-casts o progress. They sough
and strain and scour and strip richt doun
aa that reality requires. They move
as shairly as day follows nicht. They tyauve
and hunt as siccarly
as a vacuum vanquishes stour.

We lie in our beds and wonder.

Ahint the blin waas o our clenched minds
our thochts fecht and squabble wi the panic
o brattlin rats. Unsleepin and withouten speech
we hear the teeth o thon gale
ruggin at our rattlin rooves, our aiken doors.
Ticht in the daurk, we fear the force
the sichtless scrannin at our safety
our weill-steekit winnock panes.
We lie in the daurk and wonder, wonder, wonder . . .

The auld year has tellt us nocht.
It never daes.

HAUF-ROADS UP SCHIEHALLION

Well
we were hauf-roads up Schiehallion
and Michael (natch) was well in front
showin off as usual — climbin rocks
when Alasdair
turned around and said
'Whae d'ye think he's efter?
You — or Eileen?'

Well
'And what makes you think' says I
'that he's *efter* either wan o us?
EILEEN — or myself?'
I said.
Alasdair blushed.

'Well' says he 'I aye sort of
thought that Michael sort of
fancied you — only last night I sort of
saw them —
Michael 'n Eileen — sort of
back o the bothy — sort of
havin it away'

Well
I sort of sniffed — held my tongue
Alasdair grinned — and blushed again.

There
we were — hauf-roads up Schiehallion
and Alasdair turned around and said
'Well, that's aaaright!'
I could have spat! Just what in the hell
did he mean by that?

'Michael' says he 'Ye dinnae fancy him?'

Aw naw, I says
Not a bit of it, I says
Couldnae care less, I says
Here I am — HAUF-ROADS UP PIGGIN SCHIEHALLION
Aa for the guid o my health!

Douglas Dunn
THE GENERATIONS

All the young men who ever came from Inchinnan
Play football this evening on washed stubblefields.
And white-faced mothers at council-house windows
Open their windows and shout to the fields,
'Come back to this part of the country, our neck of the
                                                    woods,
We miss your habits and disapproved-of fashions,
How you lounged at the corner and smoked and swore,
The joiners and plumbers among you, the motor-
                                                    mechanics,
The shipyard workers and merchant sailors,
The boys who never came home from the wars,
Tyre-makers and farm labourers, layabouts, poets,

25

Actors and moulders, the one who was drowned in the
                                                 Gryfe,
And one in a car, by the post office, the emigrants.
Whatever you did, we know how you started.'

And all the young women who ever came to Inchinnan
Walk out of the woods and are pushing their prams.

THE GRASS

In a summer and its grass,
So long we lay in it
That the grass, withering around us,
Took away wildflowers

And stopped the droning bees.
And the grass, withering around us
To a textile bleach
Warmed us, lived with us, covered us,

We were its pasture,
The grass was our contentment,
Withering around us
Under the turbulent sun.

Be still, and be not dead.
And when we stood up,
Out of the withered grass,
The world was before us, on its knees.

Geoffrey Fraser Dutton
PERQUISITE

Along the coast
Bay rhymes with bay
Adequately;
Metres knock
To wave drop
Yawn of wrack
Roll and snore
Of reefs: no rock
About the shore
But trembles to

26

That easy power.
Foam rides upon
Deep lurchers; oar
Intrudes with caution.
Put the boat about.
Fish enough
For two we've got
Out of the wealthy sea;
Or if company's sought
Enough for three.

GROWN UP

Three hundred ton of stone
Each time, and its exploding
Dust. And so has gone
Kirk Wynd, and Caddengait,

Unravelled to a lurch
And ashes, blown
High over shouting children
Every afternoon.

Tam Gow's in that.
He drives a truck
And grins at them: looks great
In a yellow helmet.

TRYST

You'll come along the road tonight
As usual and we'll go
Not by the river down to the bridge but up
The hill. It's time you learnt
Astronomy, I'll point

Andromeda and you can lean
Against my shoulder, we'll
Parade the galaxies and I'll be brave
In the scent of your hair, quite safe
From the light-years. By the gate

Today I saw a leveret dead,
Its eyes pecked out. The crows

Watched from above. Its paws lay stretched before it.
They were red
With trying to rub away the darkness.

NEW HOUSE IN THE COUNTRY

I hear black waterfalls
Cauldron the horned mountains;
Small ferns hide in their roaring,
Rocks tremble about them.

In autumn they move downstream,
Closer. Rivers slip past us
Silently, ash trees are green;
But it's best that we leave the garden.

The mortar has scarcely set,
Timber still tangs of its planing,
Boards bang tight underfoot
And a door swings open, framing

Plaster gold in the sunlight.
This will be our bedroom.
Its window watches the gate.
It will be hung with white curtains.

Richard Fletcher
SERENADE FOR TUBA

Come up and greet my jolly golden solace.
Through here. She voices best in gurgling bathrooms.
Stroke — she won't bite — her close-coiled, shining
                                        cloisters . . .
A gin-crazed plumber, in to fix the ball-cock
swooned when his gaze rolled round her crocheted
                                        pipings . . .
Your smile leers massive, from burnished haunch reflected.
Fondle her foghorn face. I think she likes you.
Sit! Sit! I'll clasp her close and get her going.

I fell for her, my hippo, in a junk-shop.
She squatted, three-pound-ten, a chubby bargain.
A friendly welder patched one tattered buttock . . .

Ignore choleric thumps from upstairs neighbours.
My rondos resonating with their windows
enrage her cat which claws his potted cacti.
Ex- R.A.F., his tracer drills my ceiling.
Give him his way, he'd melt her down for bullets.

Have suitors, faint as simpering glockenspiels
stitched frills to hot-eyed love with lace flutes needling,
entombed their caverned lusts in lowing cellos
or scraped and sidled with seductive fiddles?
I, triple-tongued and three crooked fingers pumping,
lips firm with lung in heartfelt syncopation
will plight a fat-cheeked troth that shakes the sternum.
Our mammoth blasts bring hearts' defences tumbling.

Lips purse. Trial puffs fan distant, dripping cellars.
Stirred echoes faintly wander spiralled sewers . . .
This melancholy mastodon of music
fair uses up the brasso, I can tell you . . .
Now eggs of sorrow in her tin bowel hatching
trundle her ghostly, subterranean gloamings,
soar to the flaring spaces of her belfry.
And OOMPAH roars its challenge to despair.

Robin Fulton
WAKING IN THE SMALL HOURS

After such dreams, to land just here.

Half asleep, I count defences. First, the sea
around the island. Second, the forest around the house.
Third, the house around me. I lie thinking
of forest paths, telephones, doors opening and closing.

Half awake, I pull aside the curtain and look
up: white sky, black forest edge.
Up and up. I think of the piled constellations.
It feels like leaning over the edge of a high tower.

Reality, so plain and inescapable.
I leave it again without noticing I'm gone.

HOME THOUGHTS

If I were to return now after
'an absence'? But while absent I have gained
too much presence. It's where I live.

I add years, change houses, keep
track of myself. I post letters to the past
and answers come, always up to date.

The generations are always catching up.
The tall historic houses will still be leaning
forward like runners waiting for the starting-gun.

It's dusk — but for a pin-hole in the clouds:
a ray of sunlight glares on an empty field.
Something I can't see is being interrogated.

MUSEUMS AND JOURNEYS

An exhibition: a hundred years of Edinburgh life.
Coming out I move as heavily as a diver
on the ocean floor: one step, one breath
against the weight of the invisible dead. So many
yet the air is clear. And they've no time for me,
their view of the future blocked by giant headlines.

A journey: one I didn't want to take but took
shutting my eyes — a child again hoping the needle
wouldn't hurt. Lakes and forests, lakes and forests
pass with the weightless ease of delirium. So many.
My view of the past stays clear but hard to read
like a radio-map of a secret corner in the night sky.

Museums and journeys. We meet as strangers do
at the end of long ellipses over continents.
We exchange histories. Our view of the present is clear
but the landscapes go on sliding past. So many
memories, I try to say 'One at a time!'
They keep piling up like urgent unanswered letters.

REMEMBERING AN ISLAND

'Island
what shall I say of you, your peat-bogs,
your lochs, your moors and berries?' Strange words
to remember on a Stockholm street-crossing — it's like
a dream where you find a door in a solid wall.

North-east east and south-east
a top-heavy pile of thunderclouds,
west over Kungsholmen a glassy fire:
between, the city is a Dutch masterpiece,
still-life with evening traffic-flow.

And not a dream. I know where the walls end
and begin again. I touch doors on time.
The Highland roads in my mind have been redeveloped —
a few old curves still visible, like
the creases in my birth-certificate from the thirties.

Valerie Gillies
QUALITY OF NORTHERNNESS

India's every dawn
never differs,
flashes out by appointment:
except, seasons are wet
or not,
or have plenty of south in their gale.

The same dance
and the same chant
is danced or chanted
to the rising sun
by the millenium.
If you want a different dawn you'll be lucky.

Just once
my morning had it all,
the all of every cardinal
compass-point there is.
Cold white mists wandered
you and I up against the back of the palace.

By mistake
her white residence
reared up at us:
a newly dead queenmother herself,
this Yuvrani wrapped in stiff shawls
was signal of our extreme southernness.

She had the flap of abandoned sails.
An interior deserted:
ruinous dancing hall,
staircase treacherously fine,
lengthy mirrors telling stained truths,
cabinets emptied of english porcelains.

Only white pillars on the outside
lasted to be solid; daybreak was no
longer the warm sacred swan of self-possession
floating south and south on a lotus dawn;
it was, instead, a white icy ship
whaling through an arctic sea.

The prow of somewhere cooler
hove to at dawn
to break and sink us like icefloes:
whatever northernness was in that graveyard,
it buried us north and south
like a believer does a dead blanched heretic.

Duncan Glen
THE RIVER

The makar stauns alane
without feres
and desires the river flowin past
as me you.
A faur-gone Clyde I ken wi mysel
wi watters come frae sources
or burns or God kens whaur —

and that jaup thrown by risin trout
or drappin stane. Whaur does it gae
nou it's come and's gaein?
Whaur does it come out?

We maun staun heich in the river and tak the watters
flowin by as nou.
                    Our present taen wi joy.

We hae a new pettern formin unkent
and yet the body steerin the ripples
mair nor it thinks
for aa the strength o the flowin currents.

Dams are there to be made wi body and mind
and watterfaas creatit for our pleisure. The stane thrown,
and trout loured
wi a weill-dresst flee
if sometimes lowpin for the fun o it
                              it seems
                                    — to our joy!

The river flows on
for aa it is ours in the watter round us
— and has to be focht for.

Doun to the sea it drives
for aa our savin diversions
and is here to staun against
and feel the clean new currents
on our bodies.

But the new-formed patterns hae to be seen
apairt frae the rinnin tide. Mindit,
and guidit, upstream and doun
till raised new abune the rabblement of the watters
that whisper mony sangs at aince
o past and present. On the faur bank mony voices jaubber
and rise ane agin the ither. I staun mysel,
alane, yet at ane wi the present river.
I'm struisslin agin the tellin currents. I brace
agin strang races rinnin for stagnant creeks and pules.
Lie agin broad watters lined wi sma waves
pushin for weirs sterile for aa the reemin watters. And
yet aa aten up in the movin pattern.
A warld raised abune the river
and new and passed on
                    — if aye flowin into new watters.

33

B

We can jine haunds across the river
and feel the tide rise on us thegither
for aa we are oursels
and unique in the flowin river
each new day.

I turn again to you, as the river, and we splash
in the clear blue watter . . .

              and shout wi joy . . .

'THE HERT O SCOTLAND'

I hae problems.

I would scrieve o Scotland
and mak a unity o it

but
ken nae word o Gaelic
though I've had three fortnichts in the hielants
and went on a boat to Lochboisdale
wi hauf an oor ashore. In Inverness I was that lanely
I went to bed early. In Fort William it rained
and though I sclimed Ben Nevis in record time
it was sae misty I could haurdly see the peth at my feet.

Dundee I hae forgotten frae an efternoon visit
and Union Street, Aberdeen I've never seen to forget.
Perth I reached efter a lang bike ride
and had to turn back as soon as I got there
haein nae lichts.
Stirling Castle I hae stood on and surveyed the scene
but I mind the girl mair than the panorama.
The Borders I ken weill, enterin or leavin, by a sign
SCOTLAND
but I've never got aff the train.

I hae problems.

Fife nou is different.
It I ken frae pushin an auld bike to the limits
and stood on baith Lomonds and Largo Law. I hae kent it

early and late wi the extremes o youth. And monie
girls
but aa the faces and names nou forgotten
but ane that counts
in or out o Fife and she was born in Mallaig
whaur I've never been.
Fife is different.
I hae my Glesca voice and Fifers notice that.
And I've never played golf at St. Andrews.

I hae problems.

Still there's Edinburgh
and that gies a bit o status if no unity
for aa that aabody kens Edinburgh
(they'd hae us believe!)
I had the advantage o digs in Marchmont
and days at the Art College
— but aye a visitor wi a time limit
as still
wi sae monie ithers.

I hae problems
bein frae Lanarkshire.

It's true there's the hills by Symington
and orchards in the upper Clyde valley
and Kirkfieldbank. But
I was ane that ne'er went to see the Spring blossom
steyin put in grey streets
in the shadow o pits and bings and steelwarks.
The ugliest stretch in aa Scotland
those that ken their Scotland hae tellt us
and I anerlie kent about as faur as I could walk.

I hae problems.

There's my Scotland. A wee corner o Lanarkshire
and Glesca (I should mention!)
whaur as message boy
at fifteen I kent aa the addresses
and short cuts. There I belanged

— till I left at echteen!

W. S. Graham
A NOTE TO THE DIFFICULT ONE

This morning I am ready if you are
To hear you speaking in your new language.
I think I am beginning to have nearly
A way of writing down what it is I think
You say. You enunciate very clearly
Terrible words always just beyond me.

I stand in my vocabulary looking out
Through my window of fine water ready
To translate natural occurences
Into something beyond any idea
Of pleasure. The wisps of April fly
With light messages to the lonely.

This morning I am ready if you are
To speak. The early quick rains
Of Spring are drenching the window-glass.
Here in my words looking out
I see your face speaking flying
In a cloud wanting to say something.

Roger Stanley Green
HIPPOMENES LOSES THE RATRACE

In the canteen's clattering din
And self-service bustle I see you
And my mind blows out like a gasket as you
Park your tray near mine their plastic
Lips just touching
Beside my briefcase as usual

'Would I pass the salt' you ask
Unaware that I would pass
The escarpments of Karakorum
At a nod from your midnight brows

I grant your thin request and wish
For crystals of a richer light
Diamonds brighter than Arcturus
Sapphires more blue than Bermudan reefs

'Busy today!' you say. 'Always is,
Day before wages. Just listen
To the invoice department!'

I gaze through a veil of golden
Stars and see my phantom
Colleagues enveloping
The shepherds pie and hear
Beyond the dutiful munch
Of clerical mandibles
My heart burst open
With inner voices
Of sunlit waterfalls and
Singing birds of paradise

'See you!' you say, by way of
Valediction and plunge back
Into the typing pool leaving
A desert in the clattering room
And soon the greasy dishes will be
Cleared from round the oasis
Of this poem

'Spurs should come out on top, Saturday,'
Shouts Bunshaw watching me scribble
That's more than I will, I think
Seeing the moon fall behind the
Ivoried temples of whispering Atlantis
And I slip the remains of her applecore
Into my briefcase as usual

TO A PEEVISH WOMAN

You occupied the royal suite of my soul
And complained of draughts
You held the keys to all the doors
And let them rust
You had a ringside seat at all my contests
And kept throwing in towels

You watched the dramas from the wings
I couldn't hear the prompter for your catcalls
The tears that arose to obscure the scene

Were too salty, they would spoil your make-up
You viewed my universe from a planetarium
And thought the constellations ungainly

Together we rehearsed the music of the spheres
But you required a descant from others
The ripening diapason which engulfs
The sunset splendour which unites
Filled you with fear of harmony and the dark
You switched on artificial noons

Lady, you would ascend the staircase of heaven
And discover cobwebs at every baluster
You would find the robes and coiffures of the seraphim
Hopelessly out of fashion
And you would look around Creation and declare
That God had delusions of grandeur

Robin Hamilton
THE SEMIOLOGICAL INVESTIGATIONS OF THE [ELEC-
TRONIC] MOUSE IN THE WAINSCOATING

He lived on radio waves among the plastic furnishings.
He once acted as a sniffer-out of illicit wavelengths for
                                                        the CIA.
He listened to and occasionally retransmitted broadcasts.
His guts were a length of broadcasting wire.
He wasn't often seen and then only on purpose.
We called him Smartalec as that seemed to humanise him
                                                        a little.
He used to perch on the cradle by the baby's ear and out
    of his nose came sound and in his eyes the baby learned
                                                to beware of advertising.
He had a nervous time when he first ran out of program-
        ming, but soon came to depend on the learning-factor
                                        which had been built into him.
He once crossed the Atlantic on a stratojet and for a time
                                        was adviser to the President.
His scream was the sound of electric guitars, and when he
    whispered, you had to decode the high frequency waves.
He talked in Algol and Fortran to the household computer,
    and taught it compassion and humanity and even a little
                                                        humour.

He once became drunk on a pirate commercial station and
    spent five hours explaining that he was the illicit son
        of Marshall McLuhan.
When he died we closed his eyes with a light pencil and
    tied two used dry-cell batteries to his hind legs and
    wrapped him in a copy of *Time/Life* and dropped him
        down the garbage chute.
We occasionally hear his ghost speaking from the unmanned
        satellites among the stars.

SAPPHO

1.
I detest men, their constant spiralling to the centre.
Can they never free their minds of the lust for that vacancy
They seek within us, or see our bodies as other than
        groupings
Around that negative dull hole? The hoarse pressure
Of their demands is always with them.
Their hands already fumble in my gown, as
They decorously greet me for the first time.

Anguish wrings my heart when I look on her
And I can call to mind no image of comfort
For she is besotted with an alien kind, with man,
Even man, who lays his hand like a benediction
On the world and it burns, it burns through and through:
And where that hand has rested, only ashes remain.

This mind he brings to love twists and turns
His girl in his fancy till she, straight-laced
In the image he has preconceived, itches in every
Pore but still tries to fulfil his bonded longings.

They demand our unrestrained devotion, but their eyes
When they look at us are skinned like a dead cat's.

Is it not enough that they lay their bodies on us
But they must also lay their determined minds
Like a rigid constraining net across the world?

The flawless plastic boys' faces I pass without desire;
Narcissus' flower juts behind the ear of each of them.

39

Their eyes see only themselves, and themselves in each
                                                    other.
They turn to us with a sigh and condescension, as necessary
For the purpose but not, oh never, the best. Always
That blurred vision of the self lies in their eyes.
Their taste runs to her who returns the most perfected
                                                    image.
There is no truth and little passion in them, for they are
Truly blinded, and may not know the world as it is.

2.
The girls like apples falling from the tree
Come to me unbidden, unsought.
I teach the due decorum of a smile,
The mild eloquent pressure of a finger-tip.
At night we comfort one another with equality.
There is no she and he to breach the sweet reciprocal
Circle of our joy.

3.
Kill the hungry affectionate child
That lurks in the heart
For she will eat both milk and mother
With her appetite.
That child is hungry always and never full
Eat what she will,
Demands a love deeper than the sea-bottom,
Stronger than Ares.
Do not try to comfort that poor tormenting child,
Let her lie weeping.
Until she is still and shrivelled in a dark corner
The truth will escape you.

4.
Phaon alone among the arrogant tall-standing
I was able to love. Perhaps because he was
Born dumb. Only his hands could talk, and
In his finger tips passion had no specious gloss,
No glib remonstrance. His mind in his eyes was clear
And direct like a stork stabbing the water,
And like the lithe river fish I was speared
And carried up to him.

5.
The sad heart is at last emptied of its spitefulness.
I have given harsh words to many, but now can say no
                                                more. Anger
Came often like a teasing mist across my eyes, and
                                                through it
Both people and words rippled and twisted and became
                                                no longer
Themselves. The corruption entered them: like a mould
                                                on bread
It raced across my poems, like a flaw in the crystal it
                                                buckled
My vision of the world. Apollo will take away from the
                                                celebration
Of my history those poems, those things which should
Commemorate me. This final process of the gods is just
                                                and merciless.

Bob Harris
ISLAND MILKING

With the old cow's teats between my fingers
my forehead pressed to her moist flank
which rumbles with fulness
and gives off the past day's heat
listening to the spurt-spurt of the milk jets
she cudding rhythmically
I smelling her clover-sweet breath
for a while in the byre's half dark
we are sib the beast and I.
If I lift my head I can see
round the curb of her ribs
a mile of the sound
as smooth as her own sleek skin
and the neighbouring islands
Mull and Eilan nam Ban
like a cow and her calf
red in the afterglow
and a great round cheese of a moon
rolling off the shoulder of Ben More
into a green pasture of sky.
While the milk froths up in the luggie
warm between my knees

everything crystallises into momentary perfection
I know a little quietude
even this ache in my tired fingers feels good
even that switching sharny tail.

Tom Leonard
FEED MA LAMZ

Doon nyir hungkirz. Wheesht.

>nay fornirz ur communists
>nay langwij
>nay lip
>nay laffn ina sunday
>nay g.b.h. (septina wawr)
>nay nooky huntn
>nay tea-leaven
>nay chanty rasslin
>nay nooky huntn nix doar
>nur kuvitn thir ox

Oaky doaky. Stick way it
— rahl burn thi lohta yiz.

from IMPRESSIONS

Authentic? Joyce *authentic*? I'll tell you.
I mind well when I was about twelve, we went
to a mission. The school that is. Our Lady of
Lourdes, Cardonald. Anyway. There was this *atmosphere*,
you could have cut it with a knife. It was like the
way you felt turning up when you hadn't done your
homework, only this was a *crowd* feeling. Guilt
and terror. Awful. And this missionary was going
on about how he was fed up with boys coming to
confess about their turty habits and turty chokes.
Big pause. KATLIX ME OI! Thump. KATLIX ME OI!
                                                    Well,
anyway, I mind when I went home, my father was sitting
on the left of the fireplace, my mother on the right.
We went to the mission today, and got a sermon, I said.
What was the sermon about, said my mother. It was about
a new sin called impurity, I said. Oh, said my mother,
looking past my shoulder, it's not new . . .

Maurice Lindsay
SIGHTSEEING, PHILADELPHIA

It was to have been a purely routine visit . . .

The mother of her estranged husband, Poles
apart, they had ganged language against her.
But she found the old woman dying, mother's darling
fled, unable to face the old one's subtraction
as he had failed the young one's loving body.
Don't let me go, the old one gasped. *Don't leave me.*
Don't let them . . . as four nurses moved to open
the cancer gap with a tubeful of meaningless air.

Men with vacant faces lazily spiked
leaves and litter from Square to receptacles.

I sat on a bench, her biography of tears
telling its hurt to the clothes of a once-met stranger
she'd offered to show the town to.

                              Negresses,
bottoms steeped by high heels, nipples flaunting
braless sweaters, swaggered at corner-takers.
Under a tree, two mongrels copulated.

I sat on a bench, face brushed by sering leaves,
holding the hand of a prim librarian
who wept on my available shoulder; wept
humanity's confusion.

                              Pigeons jerked
their puffy sheen, or necked available crumbs;
squirrels lolloped nuts, were shadows traced by
the question-mark of their tails up available trees;
all of us framed in a wheeze of anonymous traffic.

It was to have been a purely routine visit . . .

by Hausen Berenze, for the Instruction of His Musicians

My work's the symbiosis of the future.
Therefore the piece consists of an arc, stretching
precisely over two two hours fifty seconds.
The arc arises out of an E and C
the orchestra reiterates in unison,
swinging from the top of the interval
to show that no arc holds finality.
This lasts for thirteen minutes fifteen seconds,
growing gradually to a climax.
Ten sections of the players then embellish
the interval in different keys
chosen by cleaners and platform attendants.
The music rises to another climax.
Thirty minutes later, the third bassoon
gets to his feet and, through an amplifier,
declaims, with swelling volume, twenty times
in varied tones, O WORLD O LIFE O TIME.
At the mention of time, the musicians break its bondage
and, for the next hour, aleatoric freedom
is given to each player. They react
as they see fit to what the words suggest.
Then, give or take a breath, the principal flautist
with his (or her) right index finger, presses
the starter button of the tape recorder.
The sounds I've plotted on a synthesiser
will dominate all else. Tubas and trumpets
leave their seats and, weaving through the players,
stand by the oboes. Wilfully they struggle
to drown the electronic oscillations.
They will, of course, succeed. The tape concludes
as suddenly as it begins. Thus, order
through freedom of expression is triumphant.
Loudly, the opening third, but now inverted,
C up to E (since every arc completed
implies the next begun) is once more sounded.
Cellists and oboeists change instruments
to signify the chaos of the wrap
of space around the order art imposes.
Then the conductor, who will have been sitting
at a locked organ consol (representing

the death of bourgeois values) must get up
on the organ bench, and through a megaphone
roar out THE REST IS SILENCE. Timpanists
advance to the rostrum, holding up their sticks
then, legs akimbo, facing the audience
beat silence on capitalistic air.
Precisely at two hours fifty seconds,
they turn and strike the leader with their left sticks
Immediately my music ceases, finished
until the next time it is recreated.

I consider applause aristocratic decadence,
since liking or not liking is irrelevant
to the new music's purpose; and to mine.
So I wish indoctrinated Marxists, dressed
like shop stewards in plain clothes, at every row-end
to quell this vulgar habit of applause.
I, Hausen Berenze, give my music,
the future's open voice, to you my sisters
and brothers who with me believe that music,
like politics, should freely be enforced.
The notes are yours, the royalties are mine.

DOWN BY THE RIVER

The river squeezed dead liquid stone
through backyard factories and mills.
A railway-bearing tunnel gulped
what once had trickled clean from hills.

Crooked in a shallow clutch, froth
rubbed off against a sedgey bank,
discarded pants, a soleless shoe,
cartons unshaped by dampness, stank

of tomcat. Rusted railings gapped
beside thin gravel. Movement, strayed
from furtive night or day, discharged
whatever need its urging made.

One isolated indian plunged
a headlong hole through gassy scum.
He made more noise, a cowboy said,
Than those blind pups thrown in by Mum.

Children that age, they vaguely heard
the distant grey-haired man declare,
are not responsible in law.
They must be taken into care.

The priest said Mass. A drunkard drank.
A pregnant belly slewed from prayer,
thankful the Blessed Virgin's gain
would give the others more to share:
while an unwanted fifteenth child
emptied its littleness on air.

HOW NOW, PROSPERO?

My ending is despair,
feigning no prayer
to offer to some god, man-made
so that it might be said.

Liz Lochhead
NOISES IN THE DARK
(Anatolia, April 74)

The four a.m. call to the faithful wakes us,
its three-times off-key harmony of drones and wails.
Above our heads I snap the lightcord but the power fails
as usual leaving us in the dark. Tomorrow takes us
who knows where. What ruins? What towns? What smells?
Nothing shakes us.
Where we touch today's too painful sunburn sticks and
sears
apart again. Faithful to something three long years
no fear, no final foreign dark quite breaks us.

Hotel habitues,
those ritually faithful wash their feet. Old plumbing
grumbles.
The tap-leak in our rust-ringed basin tickles
irritant, incessant, an itch out of the dark. Whitewash
crumbles
from the wall where the brittle cockroach trickles.
Fretful, faithful. wide to the dark, can we ever forget
this shabby town hotel, the shadow of the minaret?

Was that human or bird or animal? What cried?
The dark smear across our wall still unidentified.

HER PLACE

My rival's house
is peopled with many surfaces.
Ormolu and gilt, slipper satin,
lush velvet couches,
cushions so stiff you can't sink in,
tables polished clear enough to see distortions in.

We take our shoes off at the door,
shuffle on stocking feet, softshoe, tiptoe — the parquet
floor
is beautiful and its surface must
be protected. Dust-
cover, drawn shade
won't let the surface colours fade.

Silver sugar tongs and silver salver,
my rival serves us tea.
She glosses over him and me.
I'm all edges, all surface, a shell
and yet my rival thinks she means me well.
Oh what swims beneath her surface I can tell.
Soon, my rival —
capped tooth, varnished nail —
will fight foul for her survival.
Daughterly, deferential I sip
and thank her nicely for each bitter cup.

And I have much to thank her for.
The son she bore
(first blood to her)
never never never will escape scot free
from the sour pot luck of family.
And oh how close
the family that furnishes my rival's house.
Great succubus.
Queen bee.
She is far more unconscious,
Far more dangerous than me.

47

Listen, I was always my own worst enemy.
She has taken even this from me.

She dishes up her dreams at breakfast.
Dinner and her salt tears pepper our soup.
She won't give up.

Norman MacCaig
SEE WHAT YOU'VE DONE

I say comfortably
The core of the apple was sweet
and to hell with Eden
as I sway on my camel's back
through the eye
of that famous needle.

PRAISE OF A COLLIE

She was a small dog, neat and fluid —
Even her conversation was tiny:
She greeted you with *bow*, never *bow-wow*.

Her sons stood monumentally over her
But did what she told them Each grew grizzled
Till it seemed he was his own mother's grandfather.

Once, gathering hseep on a showery day,
I remarked how dry she was. Pollochan said, 'Ah,
It would take a very accurate drop to hit Lassie.'

And her tact — and tactics! when the sheep bolted
In an unforeseen direction, over the skyline
Came — who but Lassie, and not even panting.

She sailed in the dinghy like a proper seadog.
Where's a burn? — she's first on the other side.
She flowed through fences like a piece of black wind.

But suddenly she was old and sick and crippled . . .
I grieved for Pollochan when he took her a stroll
And put his gun to the back of her head.

FISHERMAN'S PUB

I leaned on the bar, not thinking, just noticing.
I read the labels thumbed on the bright bottles.
(To gallop on White Horse through Islay Mist!

To sail into Talisker on Windjammer Rum!)
Above my head the sick TV trembled
And by the dartboard a guitar was thrumming

Some out of place tune . . . Others have done this
Before me. Remember, in one of the Russias,
Alexander Blok, drunk beyond his own mercy —

How he saw, through the smoke and the uproar,
His 'silken lady' come in and fire
The fire within him? I found myself staring

For mine, for that wild, miraculous presence
That would startle the world new with her unforgivingness;
But nothing was there but sidling smoke wreaths

And through the babble all I heard was
(Sounding, too near, in their dreadful silence)
A foreign guitar, the death clack of dominoes.

IN EVERYTHING

Once I was on a cliff, on a ledge of seapinks,
Contemplating nothing — it was a self-sufficient day
With not a neurotic nerve to zigzag in the air.
Was that happiness? (Yes.) I sat still as a shell
Over water, in space, amongst spiders in chinks.

But suddenly I was introduced to suddenness.
As though a train entered a room, a headlong pigeon
Cometed past me, and space opened in strips
Between pinions and tail feathers of the eagle after it —
It had seen me. What vans of brakes! What voluptuousness!

What a space in space, carved like an eagle,
It left behind it! Below me the green sea-water
Wishy-washed, the blind thing, and the corally sea-pinks

49

Nodded over my hand. How can there be a revelation
In a world so full it couldn't be more full?

The pigeon hurtled out of my life. And I can't remember
The eagle going away. But I'll never forget
The eagle-shaped space it left, stamped on the air.
Absence or presence? . . . It seems I'm on a ledge of
                                                    seapinks
All the time, an observing blank-puzzled cliff-hanger.

Ellie McDonald
IN THE BEGINNING

Paradise it wis — yon glorious
acres o gowden yird, an a rowth
o flow'rs wi sic a scent
wad sair the Queen o Egypt.
Whiles i the gloamin
the Laird himsel wad cry in
for a crack an weet his whustle
wi a drappie whisky. Syne we'd hae
a lunt o baccy or a haund o rummy
tae pass the daurk Februar nichts.
I wis weill contentit
till ae day the cheil cam by
wi yon sleekit look an stertit
spierin if I wisna lickit warslin
awa on my ain an had I niver
griened for anither pair o haunds?
It didna tak muckle gumption
tae jalouse that he wis ettlin
tae wark ain o his ferlies
an forby, atween the tattie howkin,
shawin neeps an reddin oot the byre
I wis fair trauchlit whiles.
Sae I thankit him kindly;
syne he gied me the awfiest dunt
i the ribs — an there she stud —
a shilpit wee crauter wi naither
breists nor hurdies fit tae grace
the glossies lat alane the ploo.
Weill said I alow my breath

50

That cow's a ! find yersel
anither gowk tae faither yer ferlies
for I'll gang my ain gait
i the warld efter this.
Gaithered up my graith
an merched awa tae the biggin
wi the lassie traikin alang ahent.

Lorn M. Macintyre
KELTS

Spring, and the clean-run salmon
from cold northern fjords
leap in delighted recognition
of the river of their origin,
rediscovered by miraculous navigation.
In our thawing woods
shackled garrons drag
wind-blown timber
out into light,
but in deep pools
the kelts, spent fish
of an old season,
gills crowded with maggots
will gobble anything,
even bare hooks.
They lack fight.

How can the scholar
stay with his books
in the weak light
from a February sky
when the circular saw
makes harsh music
and the fly,
dancing on the water,
curtseys into the jaws
of a great Nijinsky?

Console yourself:
kelts returned to pools
will grow big,
become well mended

as the season progresses,
more discriminate
in their choice of lures.
It is how nature dresses
the hook
of the intellect,
until time strikes,
breaking strain
of the clean brain.

FOR MY GRANDMOTHER

Light and delicious
as the carrageen you whipped
in blue porcelain bowls
from fabulous Asia
these memories of you
twenty years ago
at beloved Dunstaffnage
where at the end
of the beaten track
my brothers and I
pose for the Kodak
beside the Russian scholar
while the Canadian spins
the silver dollar,
says the Yanks will lose
in Korea.

Beyond the open door
the boom of bees
where time has tossed
its keyes
in the nettles
father's slow scythe
could not subdue.
While the kettles
stutter on the stove
you buy trinkets
from the tinkers
and the slow dough
rises on a cake
for one

'nearly fifty years
a laird.'

I hold my breath
as a chill wind
spirals the snow,
blows these candles out,
and you in tears
because his great treat
is spoilt by death.

Alastair Mackie
ADAM AND EVE

In the black dark o the bed-room
the muckle ee o God —
Him that sees aathing —
looks doun
on twa bodies
his thooms drappit
rib neist rib.

Aipple ye are
and lang teen trail o a worm,
Eve-deil.
I straik your fruit
skin whaur the serpent skouks.
I tak the first bite.
Adam, dammt.

I'm smittit
wi the pest in ye.
I grou worm
and aipple baith.

He watches twa worms
fechtin.

Good or ill
we ken neither.
Like beasts
beasts o the field.

53

c

Wi the sweat o oor broo
we earn peace,
oor nicht-darg ower.

Swaalowin ane anither
in oor book
is naebody's wyte.

BEETHOVEN'S CHUNTY
'Picture to yourself . . . a rather ancient grand piano . . . Under
it — I do not exaggerate — an unemptied chamber pot.'
Baron de Tremont on a visit to Beethoven in 1809

'The chaumer's like a muck-midden.'
And he steppit atween the aidle-peels on the flair.
'It's a gey and queer rain, gin it be rain.
Herr Beethoven
maun hae a deef neb forby.'

Brakfast and denner on the cheers.
A sark sleeve plytered amang soup.
Suppin the fat
the flees joukit oot and in the soss.

On the tap o the grand piana
a smirr o stew.
Note books. A jumble o blads;
sang-notes briered atween the furs o the staves.
'The makkins o a sonata?
Mebbe a new symphony? The seeventh?'
The baron near fylt himsel to spier.

Aa o sudden he saw't.

'Losh be here!
the chunty's no been teemed!'

It stood ablow the piana,
as hamely as a joug on the brod
as the leavins on the ashet.
He'd sat on't and he'd birsed.
It haed saired its turn.

A body eats and drinks and kichs.
In atween times there's airels in his heid.
A place for ilkie thing,
ilkie thing in its place.

The baron wrote hame —
'I do not exaggerate.'

He wrote truer than he kent.

MY LATE SPRING

Makkin's like the grouwth,
thrawn.
I shoulda sawn earlier.
I mind on Horace wi his —
Solvitur acris hiemps . . .

'Snell winter lowses its haud,
it's the voar's shot noo
for braw wither and the wast winds.'

And me?

Speugs hae been at the ingan sets
the fog horn stoonds
a lane bird sings a pee-a-wallie.
Aathing's ahin.

It's my kinna spring
caulder in Lallans
than in Latin.

'Noo Venus and her bonny quines
aneth the skinkle o the moon
dirl on the yird,
ae fit and syne the tither . . .'

My Graces are doon-mou't,
my nymphs, a scunner,
my god, Pluto (colour o leed)
my leid, deid (colour o Lallans)

I shoulda seen earlier
I shoulda sawn earlier.

I mak whit I can
wi Pluto, blae laird,
his horse,
dour black brutes
plooin up the pick-mirk
nearer my mind

nor Persephone, late lass,
upskailin thro my barescrape

wi late flooers
wi late poems.

Edwin Morgan
from FIVE FILM DIRECTORS

Grierson
   Then the nets rose and fell
   in the swell. Then the dark water
   went fiery suddenly, then black.
   Then with a haul it was all
   fire, all silver fire
   fighting down the black. Then the fire
   rose in the air slowly,
   struggling over the side of the boat.
   Then it was deck and hold.
   Then it was the dance of death
   in silver with grey gulls.
   Then it was low clouds, bars of light,
   high water slapping, choppy wake
   and oilskin tea then.

Kurosawa
   Glade sword, glint running.
   Tree shiver, choked cry.
   River shadow, full quiver.
      Dust mounds, old wind.
      Grave mounds, cold wind.
   Thatch fire, child running.
   Plunder cart, thousand ashes.

Village rain, storm forest.
Storm gods, rain ghosts.
Restless fathers, prayer hearths.
Jogging banners, thrones dissolving.
Blood crop, dog pot.
    Dust mounds, old wind.
    Grave mounds, cold wind.
Cracked stave, slow crumple.
Moon blade, rolled skull.
Blood brother, spangled ambush.
Sun coins, bird calls.
Bent bow, man running.
Bent bow, body jumping.
Bent bow, neck streaming.
Bent bow, knees broken.
Bent bow, breast nailed.
Bent bow, bent bow.
Bent bow, bent bow.
    Dust mounds, old wind.
    Grave mounds, cold wind.

from TEN THEATRE POEMS

The Chorus
We have been pacing the precincts.
We are worried in unison.
We wonder what the hero is doing.
We never understand heroes.
We do not entirely believe the messenger.
The hero's mother seems perturbed.
On the other hand, the king is silent.
What is obscure is seldom clear.
We were not born in this country.
Who is that coming towards us?
Is it a man? Is it a woman?
It is the oracle. Once the oracle
has spoken, we shall be more doubtful.
In our country there are no oracles.
We are sorry today for ourselves.
But it is not for us to complain.
The king, we may say, is irascible.
Already perhaps we have said too much.

To say too much is always too often.
Here we are at the foot of the steps.
Let us all be silent in unison
and hear what the oracle has to tell us.

The oracle says, 'When winter comes
the autumn is over.' Are we comforted?
We do not know if we like winter.
We wonder what the gods are doing.
We never understood gods.

The Mask
Who am I? Who?
A false-face frog-prince, a gap-toothed witch of guisers
bobbing through smoky Halloween?
or stiff and stony gold unsmiling bearded king
of Thrace or Samothrace? a clown
above a ruff, all chalky red-spot cheeks
and eyebrows flying up like circumflexes?
a hard plain dark wood devil,
nose knocking chin, skew horns, pits for sockets?
a porcelain beauty bound with wails and flutes
to expressionless suicide? or giant ant
rehearsing its clacks and snaps,
kafka plastics rising out of jeans and hush-puppies?
In the end

you do not know who,
do not know me,
cannot ever get below me.
What is to know but papier-mache?
Even if you beat me of silver
my grace is to be inert.
My duty is to make you uneasy
as those in the caves were uneasy
when the reindeer shaman came,
or as we all feel blank
when the man walking the moon
faces us suddenly with his dark
featureless helmet.

The Fan

I make it seem and seem you see it. That's my art.
The art despises body-stockings, needs
its dark stage, pearly spotlight on the plumes,
honkytonk strains, it needs
the programmes waved as fans in the hot stalls
to be stilled. Let each eye strain.
I ruffle and quiver,
my ostrich feathers breathe
with the breasts beneath them,
I slide and flash, subside,
cross and re-cross,
wisps of plume drift off,
swirl in the tunnel of light.
I've got my dancer in my arms.
Out there, you'll never come so close,
get nipples and belly in a dream
and only as sweet as a dream thrown
on cigarette smoke and waves of heat and sound
like a screen. I am the screen
of what standing still would cheapen,
a beauty that moves and is never seen.

The Spirit of Theatre

When they set the ferret down Fred's trousers
and he pushed his head through the fly,
weaving about with his cute little bright snake's eyes,
and the women shrieked and the men
banged their beer-glasses, and the band
rolled up their sleeves for the next number —
I ordered another round.

When the finale almost but not quite collapsed
in a flurry of waterfalls and cardboard swans,
dissolving castles, two rainbows, a real
sheepdog, and a tenor merging desperately
into massed pipes and drums while the centre
microphone developed an itinerant howl —
I sighed, but sat on.

When the distinguished verse-play unwound for ever
about man's inhumanity to man

and sprayed its glacial pellets of high-grade anguish
over the culturefest, and the shirtfronts were numb
with appreciation and shushed each creaking seat,
while long bleak flashbacks crawled out, froze —
I applauded and left early.

And when I went back up yonder,
there was Shakespeare lying in wait for me.
'The mountebank returns,' he sounded off.
I could place his truculence
and it wasn't just too engaging. I yawned.
I looked at him, but all I said was
'Tongs and bones, William, tongs and bones.'

Ken Morrice
DIRTY OLD MAN

All I did was to marry
a young pretty wife.
And next day I was a father
to three children and soon
(by Christ!) they'll be married
too — the whole thing starting over.

Around us here a house
of clothes, toys, bottles,
half-written manuscripts,
other people's books,
and routine —
damp familiar taste of yesterday.

You stroll out for a cigarette
or perhaps drive down the street
watching girls as you pass.
Before you know it the war
is over and you're a dirty old man.
Someone should have told me.

The fight goes not to the strong
but to the young, to the young, to the young.

MY UNFRIVOLOUS FATHERS

I hear the dead speak.
And mind fills
with dark gods and harsh laws.

Born in grief,
schooled in old ways
of passion subdued and paradise hereafter,

moored with strong ropes
to resignation, humility, and toil —
tall masts like crosses

crowd against the sky —
flesh and family wounded
by a thousand seas,

listen now, ancestral dupes!
Hear me while I laugh and jeer.

Enfold me while I weep.

David Morrison
DAFT TAM

Whit an auld bitch she wis, the yin wha said — Puir
auld fella, Daft Tam. His mither's jist deid, and he no
able tae luk aifter himsel — he's jist a daftie onywey; a bad
lot, a troublemaker, better gin he wis deid himsel noo. —
Bit I defend ye, auld freen, and I ken ower weel that this
bitch o Hell chants the Lord's praises each Sunday in the
Wyster Free Presbyterian Kirk; typical o narrow-mindit
                                                  Scottish
so-caa'd Christianity. May the flouers o her hat perish
                                                     under
the white-shite o a skorric.
It's jist that in the hum-drum life o this toon ye send ower
monie fowk the wrang wey at the wrang time, Tam; and
                                                     ye're aye
gettin yer facts wrang, sae that the yin ye say's in jail isna
and the yin wha had it aff wi a tinker turns oot tae be the

meenister's dochter. The sherrif, e'en altho' he's a snob,
                                        didna
fin himsel in a ditch in Aiberdeen; it wis the Provost,
                                        ye ken.
Near sent him richt roon the ben that yin. The toorists
                                        ye telt
tae gang tae the Haa fir the Jimmy Shand Show were
                                        muckle vexed
that it wis really bein held in Dornach, bit never mind,
                                        ye're
aye hauf richt wi yer facts, and that fir a daftie's aye
                                        somethin.
Na, na, Tam, ye're aaricht, bit the fowk, gossips tae the
                                        core,
aye get the hauf wrang that's richt and dinna believe the
                                        ither
hauf; ach, I'm mixed up masel. Tam, ye're a constant
                                        jolt tae
complacency. Ye keep us on oor taes.
Did ye hear that that bitch o Hell wha wanted ye deid,
                                        the yin
wha chants at the Free Presbyterian Kirk, had it aff wi
the grocer in Portland Street, under the mune, oot at
                                        Ster, last
Friday, and on Sunday the Free Presbyterian Kirk
                                        meenister
preached a rantin sermon, lastin an oor, on the lustfu
                                        weys o Man.

Stephen Mulrine
from CRITICS

   Ah like a gude buke
   a buke's aw ye need
   jis settle doon
   hiv a right gude read

   Ay, a gude buke's rerr
   it makes ye think
   nuthin tae beat it
   bar a gude drink

Ah like a gude buke
opens yir mine
a gude companion
tae pass the time´

See me wi a buke, bit
in a bus ur a train
canny whack it
wee wurld i yir ain

Ay, ah like a gude buke
widny deny it
dje know thon wan
noo — whit dje cry it?

Awright, pal, skip it
awright, keep the heid
howm ah tae know
yir tryin tae read?

Robin Munro
COASTAL VILLAGE

Between the Reath of wheat
and the caring harbour
braes resound in harebells,
dancing in drifts, persuasions
of air.

The salmon coble slides in, slowing down.
The morning slows down. (Why should
mornings hurry? Evenings arrive
in their own cool time.)
The world slows
well below the speed for dealing, right
to ripen wheat,
and grapes in the Moravian village
heavy with clover, remote
from this northern one
of the grinding mussel paths.

Our south side cottages
formed like a friendship

against the obvious gradient
with no more reason
than to be when wanted
for a time;
till the time is the reason.

'Afore my mother
or her mother's time
they were a' fishermen
here. A'thing geed by sea.'

Far out at sea the long ships,
freight and container ships,
angle towards Aberdeen.
When you pick things out that clear
the light won't last.

With all their sky blue confidence
the harebell skin is fragile in a wind..
I listen to their inclination
from the sea breath rising.

William Neill
HIELANT POLISMAN

When they took away his hills
Fair Duncan of the Songs
became Grey Duncan of the Doggerel.

When the hill passes were closed to him,
the misty corrie and Glenchory
of the green grassy knowes,
they gave him a tricorn, a halberd
and hodden-grey breeches for the Sabbath day.

The prototype of Hielant Polisman
he sat off-duty in their dingy howffs,
in Canongate ingle-neuks
fisting a brandy-glass that the young spirits filled,
delighted to send a Highland poet up
to shout in Gaelic from remembered bens.

64

Why yes your honour I'll write a verse for you
sa Ghaidhlig a dhuine, is traigh na galla ort
and here's your very good health sir.

'would I were striding on Buachaill Eite
and the snow above my kneecaps
while every denizen of dull Dunedin
followed without a shoe between them'

Fair Duncan of the Songs
Grey Duncan of the Doggerel,
the fate of all bards
when time takes the hill from them.

Robert Nye
THE LONG-AGO BOY

Sometimes I meet the boy I was. He's the colour
Of lightning. He leads me
Between stoat tracks, smudged
With bright blood, in the snow,
He juggles with snowballs.

That boy lolls also in a hollow oak
Out of the sleet, and counts dead leaves
Like winnings. Up to his chin he is
In rusty guineas. He'll sniff
The pinesmoke in the candlelight
And the air on the green hill
Glorified with snow.

This friend of mine has been busy tasting the frost
Spun like candy floss about
The spokes of buckled bike.
Already he's sucked the icicles
That bristle from the eaves, and licked
The tongues sticking out of milkbottles.

The boy's ribs are bruised
By the bullying northpaw wind.
When he weeps, it's hailstones.
When he laughs, the loch gets gooseflesh.

65

The sun is bleeding to death in a puddle of slush.
O long-ago boy, let's spit at it. Tonight
We'll claw all the stars down
That dangle from Orion's stupid belt.

TRAVELLING TO MY SECOND MARRIAGE ON THE DAY OF THE FIRST MOONSHOT

We got into the carriage. It was hot.
An old woman sat there, her white hair
Stained at the temples as if by smoke.
Beside her the old man, her husband,
Talking of rivers, salmon, yearling trout,
Their dwindling waters.

A windscreen wiper on another engine
Flicked like an irritable, a mad eyelid.
The woman's mouth fell open. She complained.
Her husband said: 'I'd like
A one-way ticket to the moon.
Wouldn't mind that.'

'What for?' 'Plant roses.' '*Roses?*' 'Roses,
Yes. I'd be the first rose-grower on the moon.
Mozart, I'd call my rose. That's it.
A name for a new rose: Mozart.
That's what I'd call the first rose on the moon,
If I got there to grow it.'

Ten nine eight seven six five four three two one.
The old woman, remember her, and the old man:
Her black shoes tapping; his gold watch as he counted.
They'd been to a funeral. We were going to a wedding.
When the train started the wheels sang *Figaro*
And there was a smell of roses.

Stuart Porter
TWO GODS

In my dark ballad-land of dreams
Two gods predominate.
One — horned, dreadful,

66

Executioner of fate —
Is wild and unpredictable — the slate
Plunging from the roof,
Sudden death in a sunlit street.

The other goes on daring feet,
On tightrope over the waterfall;
Goes smilingly, arms raised, through licking flames,
Arching his lithe waist,
Laughter and wanton challenge in his eyes.

At night his finger scratches at the door;
Fearing myself, I dread him more.

John Purser
THE PIANO TUNER

Six years in training,
his right arm
achieving strength enough
to gently ease a tuning peg;
his ear dividing
cycles of sound
like slips of mica.

Then war;
plotting a submarine
in his mind's ear —
pushing aside the head-phones,
his delicate hearing spared
the perforation of death —
no need for him to rush
to the ship's side to watch
the corpses burst up to the air,
the slug's gut finding a new element,
but he was there.

Now, in the withdrawing room
he sits, pricking the felt,
the action regulated;
accepting tea only to rest his ear,
he leaves his cup half full,

tightens the strings
and keeps the hammers checked.

MUMMIFIED NUN

Closed eyelids her armorial crest,
her hair unbound, a cross is pressed
in her fingers, crossed across her chest.

Her face is creased like seaweed dried,
her belly sunken, moon and tide
leave her untouched and those full wide
breasts are spread out thin:

and written on the parchment of her skin
her fingerprint survives, the last particular,
but unidentified.

Money and title must have made
this tomb. Her whole life gainsaid
by these preserving airs. She paid

in kind, not to evade the crow's
derision or the first dull blows
of earth upon her chest. Who knows
what end she had in mind,

if end at all, — confessions of a kind
more intimate than this sad shew of flesh
in atmospheres windless and rarified.

James Rankin
COFFEE TIME

Eleven sharp they take their
Seats the ladies of the town.
They order pot of tea and cakes.
Their eyes are brightly lit.
At first a polite exchange of
Weather, then the fingers touch
The silver teaspoons.
Small waterfalls of sugar spill.

Such frail women you would
Not think could call
Up such a gale
As cool a teacup down!
They help to clear the crumbs
Away and, thank you dear, to
The waitress, thank you very much.

They smile for they know her secret
Well enough the ladies of the town.
They search for gloves,
They rise above their ruined
Confections. The girl will
Wipe the clawmarks from the cups.

Alexander Scott
GOING, GOING —

'Go,' cried the wind,
and 'Go, go, go,' cried the wind,
and the hurricane hurled me widdershins round the moon
where the dark descended,
splendid,
shattered with stars,
and made me one with the night.

'Go,' cried my heart,
and 'Go, go, go,' cried my heart,
and blood and brain were hurled in a mad typhoon
where the world had ended,
splendid,
shattered with light,
and made me one with the stars.

PRE-CLASSICAL

They call that look 'the archaic smile,'
that bliss
on faces carved before the Persians conquered,
smashing and burning,
and Athens fled from the erstwhile
inviolable city

to desperate ships and treacherous seas.

Conquest reconquered, laurelled,
return to a fresh foundation
with Pallas Athene perfect in proud marble,
but never again
that deeply secret sweetness,
that inward ecstatic
expression of inexpressible
oneness with all.

Now there were men like gods
(or gods like men),
too consciously noble
— and nubile with it.

The secret smile
discovered a dark survival
in Persian desecration,
with broken statues buried by mourning Athens
before the new temple rose
for the newly-arrogant goddess.

Her pride fell,
and followers far more haughty
went toppling too,
the Three-piece God
and Allah the Only
were aeons less than eternal.
The spade explores their wreckage.

That ancient innocence,
murdered by brute marauders,
is smiling still,
destroyed to indestruction,
recovered all its irretrievable joy.

TRUTH AND TRUE THOMAS

The wrang roads
— the 'lily leven,' the 'fernie brae' —
to hell or ferlie

gaed dounhill aa the wey
til their hindmaist end
in fire and seas o bluid.

The richt road
— 'sae thick beset wi thorns and briers' —
to grace and glory
gaed uphill aa the wey
til its hindmaist end
through fire and seas o bluid.

Here or here-eftir,
nou or in the eternal Aye,
the bluid and the bleeze
wad cleck ye in scarlet cleedin,
droun ye and burn,
for life or immortal-lang.

Was Thomas true?
He lived sae lane in a cauld country,
its lift a lour,
its sang a smore o psalms,
his makar's gear
gaed mirk as a minister's goun.

CONTRARS

Queer that the contrars, black and white,
are baith o them haly hues,
are sainit sae
wi the white Christ
and the blackenan bluid o wounds
gane cauld on the blacker cross.

Thon daith gied birth
til a rainbow revelation
on pilgrim Patmos, greenest insch
i the glenter o Grecian seas,
and heich on the hill abune the haly grotto
whaur archangel spak til saunt
frae a licht o glory
the great kirk skinkles

71

blinteran white,
a sheen to shargar the sun
and shadaw the sclent o the sea
wi a blessed bleeze
whaur the gouns o the monkish guides
are blacker nor bibles.

But nae mair black nor the Mormond braes
in mochie Buchan,
a lang lour o sterk stane
that darkens dule
abune the laigh o the land
to connach colour,
lair licht
— and yet it's ferlied yonder,
heich on the hill the pilgrim Picts made haly
the great horse skinkles
blinteran white,
to magic the mirk mountain
wi brichtness wrocht frae the blae rock
and shed its sheen as seed
to quicken the mear o the land til aa her mairches.

Thon faith had founds in fushion,
the phallic virr,
the t'ither sprung frae the spreit
nae cross could kill,
but baith o them bigged frae the licht and darkness
that howder the hert
and baith hae crottled awa frae the want o colour
in heichtened heids
that ken nae hue as haly.

But yet thae contrar colours, black and white,
are baith o them human hues
— and sainit sae?

Iain Crichton Smith
from RETURN TO LEWIS

4.

This is the place I grew in. Barefoot, I
would run to school under a summer sky
on the grass beside the road. Today I see
far larger houses each with its TV
aerial on the roof and at most doors
or in their garages new glittering cars.
The moor smells heavy as it used to do
and skylarks rise from nests. My town-made shoe
squelches among the moss. I've travelled far
from this small village by its sandy shore
with its ruins of thatched houses, roofless walls.
The girls I knew are wearing women's shawls.
The fields seem smaller, and the Standing Stones
diminished now against less wide horizons
which once were bound to simpler, slower minds.
The grass is waving now in stranger winds
and I feel sorrow more than I feel joy
as all must do who see the phantom boy
that they once were, scrambling among the pools,
in his breeze-filled jersey, or among sea shells.

5.

All night the wind blows round the house, and rain
in from the Atlantic beats the window pane.
The voices keen around me in my bed
where I shake at shadows as if the long dead
in black and green were haunting me. I feel
someone beside me under this sheet and squeal
like a rabbit in a trap. I feel my eyes
under the seagull's beak, as it swiftly flies
down through the skylight rattled by the wind.
Beneath these stony eyes I am made blind
threshing in water, and its ruinous green.
I am bewildered by this bleak machine
whose wings, salt with the ocean, flap my head
laid bare and briny on this shifting bed,
pale herring of eternity, fixed at last
by this cold sword which pierces through the blast.

Sydney Goodsir Smith
STORMY DAY AND A CAT, NOVEMBER

The gods is mairchin owre the roof
With ten-ton buits on their feet —
Valhalla houls in the lum,
Trees snap, their branches hurl
Across this high windae here . . . and
The haill world teems in a second Deluge.

I sit idle as my cat
Immobile, gazes at the interesting scene,
Intent in seeming wonder.

       ('An excellent companion for
       A literary gentleman, a cat',
       Said fat auld Gautier,
       And, Dod, he was richt, at that.)

And sae bemusit by the storm outby,
Tak ma pen to scrieve a word t'ye,
Bypittin mair important cares
Wi the full approval o' a furry cat
That maybe kens the message
That I send, my love, sweetmeat, bluid-drap —
Or maybe juist is watchin
The rain dingin doun,
Blawn by gust and squalls
And great drifts o' leaves . . . leaves . . .
A million leaves, impalpable as Paradise
       (As human dreams for us, *mon chat*)
Through the streamin windae in between, *helas!*
       (And could be richt, at that,
         Mon Theophile, n'est-ce pas?)

Nou the gods on the roof again . . .
Clump . . . clump . . . their ten-ton buits —
                Ah me!

Come on, buckle to, *mon vieux*.
Aye weill, I will. *Adieu! Adieu, cherie!*

And pray for Ptah
The Inscrutable
In Holy Egypt.
                    Enshallah!

Anne Stevenson
'TINY TUNES RULE ALL'

Wild rubbish, fine rubble and black broken windows —
six winters of hollow Glasgow and you're a wonder
of dereliction. You're sprayed and scribbled on the backs
of torn-off buildings. You're used confetti-coloured
wallpaper peeling between hearth holes and old empty
door holes. You're a bored boy with a stack of
grudges. You're sharp noses, sharp eyes
steering the Lord's disapproval through uncountable
                                                curtains.
You're yesterday's plans not completed till tomorrow is
dying. You're the clash of class against class
so reverberant your nerves burst. You're a bottle of biddy.
You're a pint. You're a sack with a thirst.
You're a sick hack dropped from the mass.
You're put out to pasture in ash. And you're broken glass.

FIRE AND THE TIDE

Fire struggles in the chimney like an animal.
It's caught in a life.
As when the tide pulls the Tay out
scarring predivtable mudscape.
Water's done knifework,
notching quick runnel and channel.

That's how you remember
the alternative lives.
You saw them, could never have lived them.
A ribbon of birds is pulled raggedly over November.
You're pulled between now and the way you will not
                                                escape.

75

BY THE BOAT HOUSE , OXFORD

They belong here in their own quenched country.
I had forgotten nice women could be so nice,
smiling beside large sons on the make-shift quey,
frail, behind pale faces and hurt eyes.

Their husbands are plainly superior, with them, without
them.
Their boys wear privilege like a clean inheritance, easily.
(Now a swan's neck couples with its own reflection,
making in the simple water a perfect 3.)

The punts seem resigned to an unexciting mooring.
But the women? It's hard to tell. Do their fine grey hairs
and filament lips approve or disdain such loving
as living alone, or else lonely in pairs, impairs?

NORTH SEA OFF CARNOUSTIE

You know it by the northern look of the shore,
by the rippled, salt-worried faces,
by an absence of trees, an abundance of lighthouses.
It's a serious ocean.

Along marram-scarred, sandbitten margins
wired roofs straggle out to where a
cold little holiday fair
has floated in and pitched itself
safely near the prairie of the golf course.
Coloured lights are sunk deep into the solid wind,
but all they've caught is a pair of lovers
and three silly boys.
Everyone else has a dog.
Or a room to get to.

The smells are of fish and of sewage and cut grass.
Oystercatchers, doubtful of habitation,
clamour 'weep, weep, weep' as they fuss over
scummy black rocks the tide leaves for them.

The sea is as near as we come to another world.

76

But there in your stony and windswept garden
a blackbird is confirming the grip of the land.
'You, you,' he murmurs, dark purple in his voice.

And now in far quarters of the horizon
lighthouses are awake, sending messages:—
    invitations to the landlocked,
    warnings to the experienced,
but to anyone returning from the planet ocean,
    candles in the windows of a safe earth.

William J. Tait

I BELANG TAE GLASGOW

Gee suzzah
nivvar kentut
wizzay sempull
tayright pohtree
onny
noohay stertut
ahdnae ken
whannay
stoap.

ASPECTS OF AIR TRAVEL

I.

    Pre-occupation with an Air Hostess

An Alp thrusts up through cotton wool:
Twin Fujiyamas strain at nylon.

II.

Barcelona Boond
(A Glesca Haiku)

Knoack'n it back abuin the cloods, an aa
Yon Fenian Wogs tae bash yet . . . Jings!

Derick Thomson
COIMHTHIONAL HIORT

Tha na fulmairean air Stac an Armainn
beò ann an carthannas,
na h-uighean a' leantainn ris a' chreig,
dannsairean air an corra-biod,
's an t-sìorruidheachd ag at
aig bun nan stalla.

Tha 'n t-sùlaire air Sòdhaigh
a' coinacraich amhaich a' ghuga,
a sùil direach air fànas,
a gob a' teagasg nan cosamhlachdan,
gach tè air a nead fhéin"

'S tha na fachaich air oir a' phalla
'nan léintean geala,
le'n guib dhathach;
mas breug bhuam e 's breug
thugam e: 'sann dh'an Eaglais Easbuigeach tha 'n treubh.'

SAINT KILDAN CONGREGATION

The fulmars are on Stac and Armainn,
living in comradeship,
their eggs keep their hold on the rock,
dancers on tip-toe,
and eternity wells up
at the foot of the rock cliffs.

The solan on Soay
fondles the gannet's throat,
its eye stares straight into space,
its beak teaches the Parables,
each one is in its own nest.

And the puffins are at the edge of the rock-ledge
in their white surplices,
with their coloured beaks;
I've heard, but don't know whether to believe it,
they're Episcopalians. Well, take it or leave it.

MO MHATHAIR

An turas mu dheireadh a chunna mi beò thu
bha t'anail air fàs goirid,
thigeadh stad ort
ann am meodhon do sheanchais,
leigeadh tu t'anail
mus tòisicheadh tu a' gàireachdainn,
agus dh'innis thu dhuinn,
facal air an fhacal,
rudan éibhinn a bhathas ag ràdh
ann a leithid seo a thigh-aire ann a Leódhas.

Ged a chunna mi marbh thu
an ath thuras,
tha do chòmhradh 'na mo chluasan,
's do ghàire,
's an cagar —
nan togadh duine e —
sinn a bhi air ar faire.

Nuair a thainig crìoch air do bheatha
thainig i cho glan,
mar gun cuireadh to snàithlean
fo d'fhiacail,
ga bhriseadh leis an aon sgobadh.

MY MOTHER

The last time I saw you alive
you had become short of breath,
you would stop
in the middle of what you had to say,
take breath
before you began to laugh,
and you told us,
word for word,
amusing things folk said
at such and such a wake in Lewis.

Though you were dead
when next I saw you,

I still hear your talk
and laughter,
and the whisper —
if one could hear it —
bidding us to be watchful.

When the end of your life came
it was a clean break,
as though you were to place a thread
under your tooth,
snapping it at a bite.

W. Price Turner
BEAUTY AND THE BEASTS

The senior lecturer is a beached whale
doubting his next breath, when told
how 'awful fat' he has grown.
Christine is taking Honours in Candour.
The trouble is, an academic male
has no way of fending sweet-sixteen
freshness of approach. He's a dead duck,
or cold condor, depending on the range,
whenever she turns up the wonder
in those quick-change stingray eyes.
Professors grow nervous when she passes,
creative fellows forget odes on urns,
and chauvenist pigs, staring away their styes,
are seized by a mad urge to cut classes.
This dainty devastator has explored
the zoo of philosophy, and declares
it disappointing; stuffed animals
ticketed in puzzle cages. Who roared
last from the jungle of pure thought?
Christine rages and despairs:
there must be some great truth not yet extinct
but they would muzzle it if it were caught.
Far from the safe hen-tracks of set print
wary safaris tackle mists. Pursuit
of meaning is a loving task, unlike
expeditions satisfied by hide
or tusk that something no longer exists.

When brute doubts muster in a snapping pack
you have to ask yourself if you are game
for untamed snouts to nuzzle in your lap.
Persist in loving truth. Try not to blame
the awkward beasts who howl to love you back.

ONLY WHEN I LAUGH

By no more light than a candle flurries
out of churning gloom, I watch my death.

It was not easy. The defenders were intent
on a long siege, with no surrender though

it doomed every stick and cushion in the place.
The fierce zest of those who held the battlements

baffled the invaders: surely so few survivors
should be quickly overwhelmed? More ladders

ringed the walls than men looked down, and on each
rung clambering armour clung thick as brambles.

Yet they fought on, tireless, cheering uproariously
at each new onslaught scattered or repelled.

The acting commander makes his final round.
Men, it is my sad duty to report that the heart

has been cut off. We now have only such oxygen
as each can summon for himself. I want

to muster one supreme response, and throw
the fear of eternity into those bastards

in the name of that beauty who sustains us all.
By her be pledged, and burn out praising!

So each brain cell rallies and glows stronger
only to contain you a little longer.

Roderick Watson
RHYMER

Let's say the sky is 'blue'
It's not enough to catch the space
The true emptiness above the hill
Cold   clear   shrill   high
The eggshell grace of the winter sky.

Call the hillside 'brown' and 'green'
'Grey' stone and 'black' earth
But words will never say the scene
The clean rock   its depth   its mass
And the yellow death of the hillside grass.

Water.   Mist.   Space.   White light.
How long to here?

Peat water is brackish brown
like tea   (write it down)   and
heather root is silver ash   old
tough   sharp   cold.

To walk miles on broken stones
A hollow path in the bones of the glen.

To rest on a bank   (True Thomas)
and to miss her   after years
a face in the pool   a high pass
the wind in the rigging of the hills.

Water.   Mist.   Space.   White light.
And how long?   Lying here?

Let's say the sky is 'blue'
It's not enough to catch the space
The true emptiness above the hill
Cold   clear   shrill   high
The eggshell grace of the winter sky.

Call the hillside 'brown' and 'green'
'Grey' stone and 'black' earth

But words will never say the scene
The clean rock   its depth   its mass
And the yellow death of the hillside grass.

PRESENT

Loss   or a sense of loss: it comes to mind
distant as passion in the stone
(the dance within the pebble)
or when my son pressed his brow
into my cheek with the fiercest wish
of bone to be one with bone.

Or late at night   distracted   mean
and restless with the radio on
stars on stars   light years stream
above us at the bottom of the well
longing   longing will find its scene
A F N   2 0 8   the Late Late Show
(a treacle well)   Oh Alice!   Oh eighteen!

Later   (since you)   days opened as simply
as a door: standing on the flint floor
of Tuscany   watching light like a tower
across a valley of olives   and vines
and dust.   Or on the shore of Ord when
we laid out fishbox ends   to spell
our names: Ullapool   Hull
Lochinver   Stonehaven.   Good times.

Tonight he slips between us in the bed
and sticks his feet into my ribs.
I hear him snuffle in his sleep.
(I have so much)   and you
are restless with another life
so: we are all here   (light years
Alice   and old rocks to keep).

Outside   the lamps turn our quiet street
to ice.   I lie and count
flashes of fire   in the darkness
of the roof   (you give me so much)

83

'These are rods and cones'   I say . . .
but the present . . .   like sparks . . .   getting away

SOME VERY OLD ROCKS — A 'FOUND' POEM
(*Science for All*, in V Volumes by Robert Brown, MA, PhD,
FLS, FRGS, author of *The Races of Mankind, Countries of
the World*, etc.)

I
The Ruler of the Solar System
Electricity
The Fall of a Stone

A Thunderstorm
Whirlpools and Whirlwinds
Ice, Water and Steam

The Bottom of the Sea
A Highland Glen
The Rainbow

II
A Visit to a Quarry
A Piece of Granite
A Piece of Whinstone
A Piece of Slate
A Piece of Limestone
A Piece of Puddingstone
Petrifactions and their Teachings

III
Flying Reptiles
The Irish Elk and its English Contemporaries
The Telephone
The Light of the Future

IV
Voyages in Cloudland
History Out of Refuse Heaps

V
Why the Sea is Salt.

84